Solitude and Silence

Solitude and Silence
The Cloister of the Heart

THOMAS À KEMPIS

Translated by
FR. ROBERT NIXON, OSB

TAN Books
Gastonia, North Carolina

Translated by Fr. Robert Nixon, OSB

Cover design by Jordan Avery

Cover image credit: *St. Bruno (1030-1101) Praying in the Desert* by Jean Bernard Restout, 1763 (oil on canvas) / Bridgeman Images

ISBN: 978-1-5051-2800-0
Kindle ISBN: 978-1-5051-2801-7
ePUB ISBN: 978-1-5051-2802-4

Published in the United States by
TAN Books
PO Box 269
Gastonia, NC 28053
www.TANBooks.com

Printed in the United States of America

"Silence can carve out an inner space in our very depths to enable God to dwell there, so that his word will remain within us and love for him take root in our minds and hearts and inspire our life. Hence the first direction: relearning silence, openness to listening, which opens us to the other, to the word of God."

—Pope Benedict XVI, *General Audience,*
March 7, 2012

Contents

Translator's Note...*xi*

Chapter 1: Solitude...1

In Praise of Solitude... 1

Mindfulness of the Goodness of God.. 1

True Humility before the Will of God 2

In Moments of Peace and Tranquility, It Is Useful
    to Remember Times of Stress and Struggle 4

Love of Solitude... 6

The Special Privilege of Solitude.. 7

Disdain for External Consolations 8

The Value of Human Spiritual Support for Those
    Who Are Struggling... 9

The Consolation of the Sacred Scriptures................................ 10

Spiritual Delight in the Company of the Saints.......................... 11

Mindfulness of Those Who Have Passed Away............................... 12

The Joys of the Person Who Is Content with Solitude..................... 13

The Virtues and Value of Community Life................................. 14

The Love of Solitude as a Sign of Devotion............................. 16

The Trials and Temptations of Devout Souls 16

The Vanity and Insufficiency of All Earthly Consolations............... 17

A Commendation of the Delights of Heaven,
    Which Abides in Jesus Christ 18
Friendship with Jesus 19
The Different Ways in Which Jesus Is Present to
    Those Who Love Him 20
The Merits of Enduring Suffering in Union with Christ 21
The Solace and Support of the Presence of Christ 23
The Life of Christ and of the Saints Was
    Not of This World 24
The Peace and Tranquility of Those Who Choose
    the Contemplative Life 25
The Secret Ark of the Heart 26

CHAPTER 2: SILENCE 29
Silence: The Protector and Guardian of Piety 29
The Example of Silence in the Prophet David 29
The Recommendation of Silence by the Saints and
    Founders of Religious Orders 31
The Virtues of Silence 31
A Remedy against Excessive Talkativeness 32
The Spiritual Perils of Loquaciousness 33
When Is Speaking at Length Useful and Helpful? 34
A Word of Caution against Excessive Rigor or Singularity
    in the Observance of Silence 36
Silence and Speech for People in Different States of Life 37
Some Particular Spiritual Snares Associated with
    Prolonged Conversations 39
The Dangers of Speaking Late into the Night 40

Bad Experiences Springing from Late-Night Conversations ... 41

Some Advice on Avoiding Conversations Which

Damage Virtue 42

Necessary Speech 43

On Turning to God Alone 43

A Consideration for the Wise.................................... 44

The Difficulties of People Who Are in the Habit of

Unrestrained Speech 45

How an Excessively Talkative Person Can Correct Himself 45

The Multitude of Vices Which Appear in Speech 46

The Vice of Detraction.. 48

How Easy It Is to Sin in Our Words and Our Hearts 48

How a Person Can Be Deceived and Retracted from the

Good Intention of Cultivating Restraint of Speech 49

Applying Discretion in Everything Which Has Been

Recommended.. 51

As a Whole, We Need to Cultivate Silence

More than Speech 51

Why We Sometimes Fail to Find Spiritual Consolations 52

How the Devil Often Strives to Impede Devotion to God

through Sadness and Boredom............................... 53

Strength and Courage Are Needed to

Overcome the Enemy 54

Appendix: Of the Love of Solitude and Silence...................*57*

Translator's Note

The following book is the first English translation of a work entitled *De Solitudine et Silentio* (On Solitude and Silence) by Thomas à Kempis, the author of the timeless masterpiece *The Imitation of Christ*. Thomas also wrote *Humility and the Elevation of the Mind to God* and *Meditations on Death*, which have been published by TAN Books. Thomas à Kempis (1380–1470) began his religious life as a member of the Brotherhood of the Common Life (a kind of religious community, chiefly of scholars and students, who lived a quasi-monastic life but without vows). Following this, he entered the Order of Canons Regular and was eventually ordained a priest. Although he did not rise to great heights in the ecclesiastical hierarchy, he was widely revered as an inspiring and astute spiritual mentor. He was also a prolific and widely-read author, with his complete works running to many volumes.

This small work presents a compilation of advice and observations on the cultivation of solitude and silence. While some of Thomas's comments relate specifically to persons in monastic or religious life, the vast majority applies to the spiritual life of all Catholics. With his customary eloquence, Thomas describes the wonderful spiritual benefits and graces which solitude and silence can confer. He also identifies potential obstacles, frustrations, and perils encountered by those who seek to cultivate these virtues, and he proposes practical and effective strategies for overcoming these.

The value of solitude and silence is affirmed by virtually all religious and philosophical traditions in the world, from the ancient ascetics of the East to the Stoics of the classical Greek and Roman world to the earliest Christian desert hermits. Within the Catholic Church, solitude and silence are central to the charism of the monastic orders (including the Benedictines, Cistercians, and Carthusians) but also an indispensable element for all those in other forms of consecrated life.

Thomas à Kempis is not, of course, advocating the adoption of a strictly eremitical life for each and every one of his readers. Rather, he recommends the systematic and intentional incorporation of solitude and silence in a manner which is consistent with each one's vocation and state of life. Aside from silence itself, he also praises restraint and moderation in speech as an admirable and neglected virtue, pointing out the multitude of sins (detraction, gossip, vainglory, profanity, etc.) which all too easily accompany imprudent or excessive talkativeness.

Undoubtedly, the cultivation of silence and solitude is an immensely valuable source of spiritual strength and nourishment for all Catholics, regardless of their particular vocation and role in the world. For it is in solitude and silence that the soul is best positioned to encounter God, freed from the multitudinous distractions of social interactions, activity, noise, images, and ideas (and, increasingly, electronic media). In the words of Robert Cardinal Sarah, "Through silence, we return to our heavenly origin, where there is nothing but calm, peace, repose, silent contemplation, and adoration of the radiant face of God."[1]

The cultivation of solitude and silence is indeed a necessary prerequisite for entrance into the wonderful experience of divine contemplation, which is the ultimate goal of all Christian prayer. This divine contemplation, the mystical "seeing God as he really is,"[2] must be considered to be a universal human vocation and not separable from the universal vocation to sanctity. For, in essence, the bliss of heaven is nothing other than this pure and eternal perception of the Divinity. This vision of God may also be experienced (to varying degrees) even in this world through the

---

[1] Robert Cardinal Sarah, *The Power of Silence: Against the Dictatorship of Noise* (San Francisco: Ignatius Press, 2017), 54.

[2] 1 John 3:2.

grace of contemplative prayer. And solitude and silence are the hallowed doors through which one must pass to arrive at this delightful and serene state of holy contemplation.

May Jesus and the Immaculate Virgin guide us safely through these portals, both by their example and by their never-failing and most merciful assistance.

Fr. Robert Nixon, OSB
Abbey of the Most Holy Trinity
New Norcia, Western Australia

1

Solitude

In Praise of Solitude

My dear friend in Christ, it is my earnest wish to provide you with a kind of small booklet to which you may turn whenever you have a few moments free from the external tasks and labors in which you are engaged. Rejoice and delight in such moments, for in them you may turn most fully to the Lord, in whom alone your true happiness and serenity is to be found!

I shall now humbly undertake to share with you some insights into the spiritual pleasures and benefits of solitude and silence, for these are ever the true friends and allies of the soul who seeks the peace and freedom which only Christ can give.

Mindfulness of the Goodness of God

In your moments of solitude and leisure when you may relax quietly and without distractions, you should always take the opportunity to reflect on the infinite goodness of

God. Consider particularly the vastness of the benefits that the Lord has so generously bestowed upon you.

Whatever you experience in this life, whether its seems to be good or bad, easy or difficult, delightful or painful, may (and should) work for your spiritual progress. If you are attentive, you will experience and discover something new each and every day, and you may learn some new lesson thereby, gaining a fresh insight into the nature of God, your fellow human beings, and your own self. Every opportunity to enter into solitude is unique and different in some way from all other such occasions. In each of these moments, you have a privileged and wonderful opportunity to enter further into the infinite and inexhaustible mystery of the Divinity and to come to understand your own nature—including your strengths and weaknesses—more fully.

True Humility before the Will of God

The circumstances and conditions of this earthly life are incessantly changing and fluctuating. Truly has it been said that nothing here remains the same. And these changes come about either through our own selves or through others or through nature itself. Yet amidst all this change and variation, this fluctuation and fluidity, we should constantly recognize the will of God unfolding itself according to some mysterious and unseen divine plan. And we should humbly pray to the Lord that whatever He wishes should come about, saying to Him sincerely, "Thy will be done," and trusting absolutely that it will ultimately assist in our own salvation and lead us to final peace and happiness.

Just as clay is molded and fashioned in the hands of the sculptor, so are we all being formed and shaped by the hands of God. The fact that God even deigns to work on us and to fashion us is itself a stupendous mark of honor and love, even when the process of being molded may be difficult to understand or unpleasant to accept. And whether God chooses to form us into some large and much-admired work of art or He makes of us something small and humble, we should not be particularly concerned or worried. For even if we seem to be the least amongst our brothers and sisters, we are still equally the work of God's loving hands. We are no less esteemed by the only One whose esteem truly matters!

And we should trust and have confidence that God holds us all in special dignity and particular and unique value before Himself. For He is a loving Father to each of us, whatever we happen to be or possess, through nature or through grace. We should, therefore, not concern ourselves greatly over differences in external merits or talents, or the apparent importance of the particular roles which we (or others) are called to perform. Indeed, we should neither feel discouraged nor dejected, nor elated and self-important. Nor should we never look down upon others who seem to be less important or virtuous than ourselves, nor should we envy others who seem greater and more gifted than we are.

Whatever the role or station in life you happen to find yourself, you may still engage fully in the most important and highest work which any human being may possibly do—which is contemplating God in love and serving Him in prayer, devotion, and charity. Whoever you are and whatever is your situation in life, we can all find some moments of solitude in which to devote ourselves to this exalted and noble calling of divine contemplation. This is the highest work of even the seraphim themselves! It is a holy vocation which is universal, and yet also most profoundly personal for each of us.

IN MOMENTS OF PEACE AND TRANQUILITY, IT IS USEFUL TO REMEMBER TIMES OF STRESS AND STRUGGLE

Whenever you are enjoying some time of peace and rest, it is useful to call to mind those times when you have been busy, overworked, or stressed. Whenever you are enjoying the calmness of solitude and silence, it is useful to reflect on those occasions when you have been assaulted with noise and activity. Indeed, calling such things to mind is a sure and effective way of learning to love and value the peaceful tranquility of your times of solitude!

If you reflect upon how easily you can become anxious or worried, or how little it takes to perturb your soul, you will also realize that the achievement of true inner peace is not something which human efforts can ever achieve on their own. Left to yourself, how often you have fallen prey to anxiety, even when there is little or no real need to worry! How often, even when you are surrounded by exterior silence, your mind is still filled with the clamor of unruly and agitated thoughts and disturbed by your own worries!

Since this is an undeniable characteristic of our fragile human nature, to experience both exterior solitude and interior peace can only be a gift from God. And God generously gives such moments to all, as long as they do not resist Him or refuse His gift. It is at such times that you should turn yourself to divine contemplation. And to the soul which enters into such contemplation, all earthly worries, desires, and distractions will soon seem to be as nothing!

But the person who refuses to give himself over to solitude and occasional inactivity but compels himself instead to be constantly busy or constantly interacting with others, refuses and resists this great gift of God. And it is, alas, a very rare thing for such a compulsively busy person to come to know the delights of contemplation.

LOVE OF SOLITUDE

"Flee, my beloved!"[1] says the soul to its spouse. For Jesus, who is the true beloved spouse of the soul, is often read to have fled from the crowds and taken Himself off into the desert places to seek solitude.

You will surely be with Jesus if you, too, flee from the crowds and seek out the "desert places." And when you find such a place in your soul, let it be as a secret garden of delight to you. Guard and protect it most carefully!

Saint Jerome compares the place in which one finds solitude and refuge from the crowd to a Garden of Eden, for he writes, "As long as you are away from your heavenly homeland, let your place of solitary refuge be as a Paradise to you." In this spiritual Garden of Eden of solitude, you will indeed rejoice in the Lord. You will converse with God, and He shall speak to you. And His glorious light and truth shall be manifested and revealed to your heart with ever increasing radiance and clarity.

Just as when the sun first rises at dawn, its visible rays are soon multiplied more and more, even so, when Christ comes to you, the interior dwelling place of your heart shall become more and more illuminated. You will be purified by a new light, and in its glorious splendor, your interior being shall joyfully exult.

---

[1] Song of Songs 8:14.

And then you shall surely exclaim, "O Lord, to whom may I compare you?"[2] And you will experience firsthand the truth of that eloquent verse of Scripture in which it is written, "In your light, we see light."[3] And again, "The Lord is my light and my salvation."[4] And, "In your light, O Lord, I will walk, and I will exult in your name, for you are the glory of my virtue, and my delight!"[5]

THE SPECIAL PRIVILEGE OF SOLITUDE

Consider, my friend, the special privilege which you have received by virtue of your situation and status in life, and exercise care to live in such a manner that you take full advantage of this privileged vocation.[6] For not all people are gifted with the opportunities to spend time in contemplation, as you are. As for yourself, you are blessed with a suitable place for prayer and chances to spend time in solitude which exceed those of most other people.

May the Spirit of Jesus be with you, for it is His Spirit alone which teaches and illuminates "all those entering the world."[7] When His Spirit is present, you shall surely

---

[2] Psalms 89:2.

[3] Psalms 36:9.

[4] Psalms 27:1.

[5] See Psalms 89:15–17.

[6] Thomas was writing this particular counsel for people in consecrated religious life of one form or another. Nevertheless, his comments here will still be found relevant for many Christians in other states of life.

[7] John 1:9.

neither need nor desire the presence of other human beings to console you or entertain you.

But when you feel that His Spirit is absent from you, then
be content to wait patiently. For He shall indeed come when
He judges the moment to be opportune and will not delay.

DISDAIN FOR EXTERNAL CONSOLATIONS

It is wise advice to beware always that you do not fall into
the habit of seeking consolation and diversions in the
exterior things of this world. Rather, strive to find your
consolation in interior silence. And when this consolation
cannot be found, then call upon God with tears of sincere
compunction and repentance, and He shall surely not fail
to hear you and answer you in the way that is best.

It is useful, however, to speak to a human spiritual guide at
times. You should honestly confess to such a guide any occasions or habits of negligence you currently have, and reveal
any anxieties which you are experiencing. At certain times,
such conversations are useful and helpful. For not all people
receive the grace to be able to echo the words of the apostle
Saint Paul, when he said, "I have been instructed by no human
being, but through the revelation of Jesus Christ himself."[8]

But to the one who finds himself to be free of the need
for human guidance and companionship—he may count

---

[8]   Galatians 1:12.

himself as being specially blessed and should thank God sincerely for the particular strength and grace he has received from Him.

THE VALUE OF HUMAN SPIRITUAL SUPPORT FOR THOSE WHO ARE STRUGGLING

But it must be acknowledged that there are many who struggle greatly with solitude and rely upon a human spiritual director to guide and accompany them. For such people, they should attentively listen to the words of their spiritual director as if they were not merely human words but the words of God communicated to them by means of a human agency.

God speaks to each of us in a way that is adapted to our needs and our state of development. Indeed, whenever necessary, He is willing even to speak to us as if we are little children, sometimes through other human beings and sometimes through the words of Sacred Scripture. We may be confident that whatever consolation, encouragement, correction, and guidance we most truly need, the Lord will never fail to provide it for us. But it behooves us to trust God's judgment in this matter and not give more weight to our own opinions and preferences.

The Consolation of the Sacred Scriptures

For those who find no encouragement or consolation in the things of the external world, Sacred Scripture shall always provide a rich source of delight. For when you read the Gospels or the prophets, do you not feel as if you are enjoying a conversation with Jesus Christ Himself? Is it not a wonderful happiness to encounter the noble apostles and prophets in their inspired writings, just as if you were meeting them face to face?

And when you read the books of other great saints and doctors of the Church, is it not like enjoying the companionship of these awe-inspiring men and women? Surely this is enough to dispel any shadow of tedium or lethargy from one's mind!

Whenever you read the golden words of Saint Augustine or Saint Gregory the Great, do you not feel like you are looking upon these men as if they were truly present to you? Their wonderful words should not mean less to you or touch you less deeply just because the writers are not there speaking these words to you in the flesh, for whenever you read their books, they are most certainly accompanying you in mind and spirit.

Spiritual Delight in the Company of the Saints

Indeed, it is possible to enjoy the companionship and friendship of all the saints, even though they are not physically present or visible to the eyes of the body. For the spiritual person realizes that all are living and present to God, who dwells in eternity. And if these saints are all living and present to God, to whom you yourself are also living and present, does it not follow that the entire communion of saints, and each saint individually, is present to you also?

Though Jesus Himself departed from the world in a physical sense so that we can no longer perceive His presence with our eyes, yet it is not to be doubted that He remains truly and everywhere present to us. For by removing Himself from our physical senses, we are able to perceive Him more truly through the interior vision of faith rather than through the limited exterior vision of physical sight. And for this reason, through faith we are able to cling to Him more closely, to love Him more dearly, and to receive His Spirit more fully than if He were physically with us, like an ordinary human friend. Thus Christ declared, "Unless I go away, the Holy Spirit will not come. It is therefore more beneficial for you that now I depart from your presence."[9]

---

[9] John 16:7.

MINDFULNESS OF THOSE
WHO HAVE PASSED AWAY

Whenever those whom we have loved and who have been faithful during their life have passed away, we may be confident that they are now rejoicing in the eternal peace of heaven. And we may be confident that, as long as we remain faithful to Christ, we are following them to that glorious place where they now rejoice.

For they have surely gone to the Father and now dwell in the celestial mansion which He has promised them and prepared for them.[10] It is to this celestial mansion—a place of ineffable light and peace—that each human heart constantly aspires during this mortal life. It is to this realm of everlasting rest and infinite joy that our souls ceaselessly yearn to fly, as long as we labor in this earthly valley of tears.

And if there are any of our beloved departed who, for some reason, have not yet gained admittance to the eternal kingdom, then it behooves us to keep them in our prayers, and similarly to offer up works of patience and charity for their sake. For by doing so, we bring consolation and encouragement to their souls, and also help to advance them in their journey as they make their way to the joys of heaven.

---

[10] See John 14:2.

The Joys of the Person Who Is Content with Solitude

There are certain people who have arrived at a state of such spiritual grace that they no longer need human companionship or support but find all their pleasure and satisfaction in holy solitude. Such people ought to rejoice very greatly at this singular blessing! For the less one depends upon exterior consolations, the more richly may one experience the interior and higher joys of the spirit.

Such fortunate people should strive to cast off all earthly cares, anxieties, and desires, and devote their minds to ever more profound penetration of the Divine Law and celestial mysteries. They should also contemplate deeply the boundless joys of heaven. For even though these joys may not yet be attained or experienced, the simple act of contemplating them brings a certain foretaste of them and is to the spiritual mind a source of constant delight and refreshment. From the holy desire for the joys of heaven, the soul will shed tears—not the bitter tears of sorrow or despair but rather the sweet tears of fervent love and ardent longing!

Thus it is that the prophetic David speaks of these tears, which express nothing but the pure desire to see God, when he says, "Tears have become my bread day and night, whilst they say to me, 'Where is your God?'"[11]

---

[11] Psalms 42:3.

How wonderful it is for a person to find himself in such an exalted spiritual state! Yet it must be admitted that to persevere like this is by no means easy but demands unceasingly diligence, effort, and carefulness. For there are always a multitude of distractions and temptations, both from outside and from within, which conspire to draw us back to earthly things and the desire for the exterior consolations of this lower realm.

THE VIRTUES AND VALUE OF COMMUNITY LIFE

Notwithstanding the admirable nature of the solitary life and the blessedness of those who are content to abide in solitude during this present life, if a person is able to be content with life in a particular and stable community, that is also a very great and commendable thing. To be genuinely happy with life in a community means to accept the conditions, limitations, and persons who form that community just as they are and not to be seeking for distractions or consolations beyond them.[12]

---

[12] It is to be noted that Thomas is addressing his advice here to persons living in enclosed religious communities. Nonetheless, what he says may also be applied to persons in secular life, since most people find themselves in communities of one kind or another (e.g., families, parishes, workplaces, etc.).

Nevertheless, it cannot be denied that many people will sometimes feel the need to have time apart from their community. This is sometimes on account of necessary business, or sometimes in response to a personal desire. And there are those who simply need to go out walking, for a proverbial change of air and scenery.

It behooves us not to be judgmental of others in this regard but to be tolerant of human weakness. For there are those who abandon religious life altogether when they come to find it excessively tedious and come to feel that its burdens are too much for them to bear. Hence it is best to order all things with gentle moderation in accordance with human limitations and the grace God bestows on us. This does not prevent anyone from aspiring to the highest and strictest ideals of religious life, but these must be approached with humility, realism, and patience.

For this reason, I encourage you to cultivate solitude and silence diligently but not obsessively or tyrannically—in a way that is in accordance with your own true personality and which takes into account your various limitations and potentialities.

THE LOVE OF SOLITUDE AS
A SIGN OF DEVOTION

It is a sure sign of devotion to God to love with real affection the solitude of one's own cell,[13] or some other place where silent mental prayer or contemplation are able to be undertaken freely. Such places are of value because they allow one to pray and to elevate one's mind to divine contemplation without distraction from other people or external things. To the one who is truly devout, the life of prayer and contemplation should be tranquil and delightful, not burdensome or dull.

Similarly, to the truly devout person, *any* occasion or location can be suitable for engaging in contemplation and prayer, and all time given to these activities will seem to pass by quickly and easily.

THE TRIALS AND TEMPTATIONS OF
DEVOUT SOULS

Despite all this, many genuinely devout people have experienced severe trials and temptations. Often the activities of contemplation and prayer seem to cease to be sweet and delightful but become bitter and boring. When this happens, such persons should not be quick to abandon their

---

[13] A cell refers to the room in which a monk or nun sleeps, prays, and reads, etc.

practices of devotion, nor should they imagine that God is for some reason displeased with them.

Rather, they should call to mind that it is, in fact, useful and salubrious for them to undergo trials and deprivations at certain times. For it is only by undergoing battles that victory is won, and only through labor that rewards are earned. It is through suffering and endurance of difficulties and dryness that true patience is cultivated. Moreover, such experiences help to teach us to be compassionate and tolerant towards others, who may be undergoing similar spiritual experiences.

The path to eternal life becomes more glorious and meritorious when it passes through trials and temptations rather than when it is uniformly quiet and tranquil. And bearing suffering, not taking one's ease in comfort, is the surest way of achieving the spiritual perfection to which we should aspire. This is something well illustrated in the life of Christ Himself and the lives of all the saints.

The Vanity and Insufficiency of All Earthly Consolations

What do the passing and momentary pleasures of this mortal life profit the human soul, since they are all here today but gone tomorrow and fly away from us even as we attain them? None of them can be grasped or retained permanently or securely. Or what created thing is possibly able to give more happiness and satisfaction than the Creator Himself? It is true that we may sometimes use the beauty and wonder of created things to lead our minds to ascend to the glories of the Creator. But if we seek the pleasures and beauties of created things as ends in themselves, our soul will inevitably be left disappointed and unsatisfied.

It is true that our love for the Creator leads and requires us to love certain created things (such as our fellow human beings) in an appropriate degree and manner. But the delights arising from the lower desires of the flesh (which are sometimes mistakenly called loves) are always contrary to the true progress and peace of the spirit.

A Commendation of the Delights of Heaven, Which Abides in Jesus Christ

My friend, let your soul take the time to contemplate the beauty of your heavenly Spouse,[14] and consider the exalted nature of His love for you. And know that whatever or whoever you love except for Him shall never completely satisfy or fulfill you. Rather, anything else you might choose to love will, in the end, prove to be inconstant and will flee from you like the passing moment. For nothing in this life lasts forever.

---

[14] That is, Christ, who was considered to be the spouse of each soul.

Indeed, all earthly glory and fame is fleeting. Very often, it delivers only bitterness, sorrow, and disappointment to those who would court her. And this finite and passing world offers nothing that can truly satisfy the immortal soul, which is made in the image of the infinite and eternal God.

But Jesus alone, who is Himself this eternal and infinite God, offers to us an ineffable sweetness and unfathomable delight. During this mortal life, He visits the faithful heart and bestows on it the consolation of inner peace and tranquility; and in the future life, He will fill the soul with the miraculous and transcendent beatitude of God Himself.

FRIENDSHIP WITH JESUS

Therefore, seek to be enriched with the consolation of Christ and to be refreshed with the secret sweetness only He may give! For He has declared, "No one comes to the Father except through me."[15] There is no place so lonely, nor solitude so complete, that Jesus is not already truly present there to those who love Him. Hence, to be in solitude is always to be with Jesus.

Without Him, every place always becomes tumultuous and stormy. But whenever He is there, every place and every circumstance can be a refuge of peace and delight. It is sweeter to be with Christ on the cross than to be without

---

[15] John 14:6.

Him in paradise! And if Jesus is present, what else could possibly be desired?

The Different Ways in Which Jesus Is Present to Those Who Love Him

Christ is indeed present to us now, but in a manner which is congruent with our current state of existence as pilgrims and exiles. For it is only after this earthly life has ended that we shall see Him fully, as He really is. Christ is always present to us, but not always in the same way.

For sometimes His presence is revealed through the sufferings and trials which we undergo. But other times, in contrast, He is present through the removal of the adversities we face and the restoration of peace. He is present in this way to those who love Him, but never in such a way that they are freed completely from all adversity and pressure. For He has truthfully declared, "In this world you will suffer tribulation."[16]

His presence to us may be compared with that of a good father to his offspring. He disciplines us but never kills or destroys us. He sometimes seems to leave us for a while, but only so that we may learn to support ourselves and to have courage and faith; for He never truly abandons us. We sometimes suffer from hardships or are burdened with troubles, but never so much that we are actually broken or

---

[16] John 16:33.

crushed by them. We may sometimes experience sorrows and deprivations, but this is only so that we come to long more eagerly for a better world, the world-to-come of heaven. Indeed, in this way, we learn to love that which is eternal and unseen and to regard with detachment everything that is passing, visible, and earthly.

Christ is present to His faithful in bestowing grace, in providing interior consolation, in revealing heavenly mysteries, in granting peace to the mind and body, in overcoming vices and passions, and in resisting temptations and trials. But at certain times, He permits these blessings to be removed or concealed and adversity and hardship to befall the devout soul. For it is by these means alone that faith is tested and made stronger and purer. This faith is indeed "more precious than gold, which is tested by fire."[17] But nevertheless, Christ is truly present during those difficult times, even when He seems to be absent. For, in the greater scheme of things, it is precisely those times of difficulty and trial which prove most useful and fruitful for our spiritual growth.

THE MERITS OF ENDURING SUFFERING IN UNION WITH CHRIST

How blessed and meritorious is the one who loves God just as ardently and faithfully in the midst of adversity as in the

---

[17] 1 Peter 1:7.

midst of prosperity and peace! Blessed indeed is the one who is just as happy to go hungry and thirsty in the company of Jesus as to enjoy a sumptuous feast with Him! Such a faithful soul is ready not only to follow Christ to the glory of the mount of the Transfiguration but also to follow Him to the grim hill of Calvary and to the torments and shame of the cross. Such a faithful disciple of Jesus proclaims his Master to be great and glorious with all his heart in all these changing circumstances, whether they are good or bad.

Hence it is that Jesus declares in the Gospel, "Blessed is the one who does not fall away from me."[18] He said this because He knew very well that adversities and tribulations of one kind or another are bound to come to all His disciples. For it is not in times of peace and prosperity that the strength of our faith is really tested, but in times of difficulty and struggle.

My friend, love Jesus when He bestows blessings and good things upon you. But love Him no less when He takes these blessings and consolations away, or even sends you tribulations. Let nothing whatsoever—neither success nor happiness, neither distress nor suffering—separate your heart from your Savior!

Indeed, it is when our fleshly or merely human nature suffers or is hurt that we have the opportunity to teach that very nature to be obedient to our spirit and our reason.

---

[18] Matthew 11:16.

And it is in this higher spiritual dimension of our being that the truest and most pure love abides.

The Solace and Support of the Presence of Christ

Wherever you go and whatever you do, let Christ be present with you. Abide always in His holy company, and seek His wise counsel and advice before you make any decision or undertake any task. And beware that you do not stray from Him or offend Him in any way. For if you separate yourself from the one who is the Prince of Peace, what peace may you then expect to enjoy?

Ambitious thoughts and immoderate elation and love of earthly pleasures and enjoyments all serve to dull the vision of the mind and to cloud the eyes of the heart. The person who permits himself to be rendered dull and blind by the illusions of this passing world ceases to see the Lord Jesus, either enthroned in glory with the Father or as a tender babe in the presence of His immaculate Virgin Mother in the stable.

Those who seek consolation and diversion in material and worldly things soon lose their taste for that which is spiritual, in the same way that a person who indulges in coarse food or wine loses the ability to appreciate that which is fine. To such a person, devotion and contemplation will began to seem insipid and tedious. One form of desire and love always drives out another one, which is (so to speak) its rival. Thus, conversely, it happens that the person who seeks his delight and satisfaction in spiritual things alone will soon come to disdain and abhor all worldly and fleshly allurements.

THE LIFE OF CHRIST AND OF THE SAINTS WAS NOT OF THIS WORLD

The life of Christ goes before us as a radiant beacon and example of virtue. All the saints also present us with wonderful exemplars, for they all emulated Christ in their own particular way and setting. We see that Christ, together with all the saints, was not fascinated by the desire for fine or fashionable clothes, nor gold or silver, nor precious stones, nor abundance of wealth. Not one of the saints was devoted to extravagant feasting, or the pleasures of the flesh, or human popularity.

Indeed, the comforts and delights of the body could not seduce their hearts; nor perfumes and scents capture their nostrils; nor could visible beauty enslave their eyes. For they all realized, both by divine illumination and by natural wisdom, that the pleasures and joys of this world all pass quickly, together with earthly life itself. Our hope for eternal and substantial joys is, therefore, not here but in the realm which lies beyond this life. They all perceived the vanity of earthly pleasures and the madness and foolishness to which the lusts of the flesh so easily give rise. Of these, it is much better to be silent than to speak about them, or even to think about them! For merely reflecting upon or recalling the pleasures of the senses can be enough to pollute and distract the spirit and to damage the purity of one's innermost heart.

The Peace and Tranquility of Those Who Choose the Contemplative Life

You who have chosen the contemplative life are indeed blessed, for you have spurned the tumult and snares of this deceptive world and fled to the protection of the Lord Christ. There, beneath the shadow of His wings, you will find peace and repose. You have indeed chosen wisely in determining to live your life directed to Christ alone, and concerning yourself with how you appear before Him only.

If you love Christ and the blessed Mother of Christ, and if you follow diligently the example of the saints who similarly loved Christ and His dear Mother, no other love will be able to enslave you or deceive you or capture your heart. Neither the cares of the flesh nor poverty of material goods nor burdensome labor nor solitude and silence shall be difficult to you. On the contrary, in loving Jesus and doing all things for love of Jesus, all things will become delightful!

THE SECRET ARK OF THE HEART

My friend, I urge you to fashion for yourself an enclosure or cloister inside your heart so that—wherever you happen to be or whatever you happen to be doing—you have a place of solitude hidden within yourself.

Build this interior chamber of solitude like the ancient ark of Noah so that whatever floods of water this wicked and inconstant world may rain upon you, you shall remain always safe and dry. Think of John the Baptist, who stood upon the banks of the river Jordan and raised his eyes to see Christ coming to him. You, similarly, should stand on the banks of the turbulent and perilous river of this world and raise your vision to Jesus! The ark which you build in your heart should have but one entrance so that you may guard it diligently. Let Christ enter in, but take care to shut out the devil and his multitude of minions.

For the wicked devil is the incessant enemy of all those who are good or who aspire to become good. And he is particularly envious and inimical to those who pursue the contemplative life. The more one progresses in the life of the spirit, the more bitterly does the devil attack. Let us arm ourselves against his fulminations and his fury. And may we know the strong protection of our Lord and Savior, Jesus Christ; to whom be glory forever and ever. Amen.

2

SILENCE

SILENCE: THE PROTECTOR AND GUARDIAN OF PIETY

It is not sufficient, my friend, that you learn to esteem and enjoy solitude, unless you also learn to love its companion, silence. For silence serves as a protector and guardian of piety. Through the inability to refrain from conversation at certain times, innocence of heart can easily be sullied, and our holy intentions can be undermined.

THE EXAMPLE OF SILENCE IN THE PROPHET DAVID

It was for this reason that it is written of holy David, who came to contemplate and to proclaim so many celestial mysteries, that "Chusi was the friend of David."[1] Now this name, Chusi, means "silence" in the Hebrew language.

---

[1] See 2 Samuel 16:16.

This close friendship between David and silence is reflected in many verses of his psalms. For example, he writes, "I said, I shall guard my ways, lest I should stumble through my tongue."[2] And a little later he writes, "I was mute and humble, and I kept silent even from good words."[3] In another instance, he implores the Lord to grant him control over his tongue, saying, "Place, O Lord, a guard over my mouth, and set a secure gate at my lips."[4]

David was such a great and wise man that he was deeply loved by the people and many nations came to be subject to his rule. And he loved silence and placed a metaphoric guard over his lips, and humbly prayed to the Lord to grant him restraint over his speech lest he should be overcome by weakness or flippancy and let ill-chosen or imprudent words escape from his mouth.

Where, may one ask, did that ancient king and prophet learn this key principle of religious life? How did he come to know this cornerstone of the Christian monastic charism? Certainly, it was only the grace of the Holy Spirit which instructed him in the value of silence and the wisdom of its careful cultivation. If this same Holy Spirit is truly with us today, we also shall learn to love silence as a guardian of virtue and seedbed of wisdom, just as it was esteemed by the holy patriarchs and prophets of old.

---

[2]   Psalms 39:1.
[3]   Psalms 39:2.
[4]   Psalms 141:3.

The Recommendation of Silence by the Saints and Founders of Religious Orders

Virtually all the founders of the various orders of monastic and apostolic life have commended silence strongly, and all the saints have both exemplified and taught this practice. There are many—such as monks, nuns, hermits, and members of religious orders—who are required to observe silence for certain times each day as part of their daily conduct of life. But even those who are not canonically bound to such an observance will find that it is a wonderful practice to adopt. It is assuredly the source of great merit in the sight of God to commit oneself to refraining from conversation and speech at certain times each day.

And not only will it promote virtue, moderation, and self-control within yourself, but it will also serve as an edifying example and positive influence on others when they see you adopt (of your own free will) certain aspects of the stricture of religious or monastic life.

The Virtues of Silence

If you are diligent in the practice of silence at certain times, you will discover a multitude of virtues hiding within this simple act of self-restraint. For by silence, you will retain humility and will adorn yourself with modesty. For keeping silence implies deliberately refraining from making a display of one's own real or imagined merits, cleverness, and insights before others. It is a way of showing respect and obedience towards others by being more ready to listen to them and to defer their judgment. Silence is also an effective way of promoting peace and harmony within a community.

You shall find that silence will serve as an invaluable protector and guardian for you if you keep the strictest silence at all times when this is required or expected of you. And even when it is permissible and acceptable to speak freely, it is useful to say only what is necessary or useful to others in some way rather than talking merely for self-gratification. Whenever you find yourself saying something purely through flippancy or boredom or carelessness, endeavor to correct yourself at once. And take note of the occasion and direction of your imprudent or thoughtless speech so that you may avoid similar instances in the future.

A REMEDY AGAINST EXCESSIVE TALKATIVENESS

An effective remedy against a tendency to excessive talkativeness is to refrain from speaking even when it would be perfectly permissible and acceptable (and even beneficial) to speak. In this way, the discipline of restraint of the tongue is specifically and intentionally trained through a deliberate act of will.

It is the wise student who does not wait to be correct-
ed or punished before he recognizes when he has made a
mistake. In the same way, a person should frequently ask
himself, "Am I talking too much?" rather than waiting for
others to point it out to him!

The Spiritual Perils of Loquaciousness

If a person is accustomed to speaking each and every time
he has the opportunity to do so, when shall he be free from
words in order to be tranquil and still within himself? If a
person is excessively talkative, he will not fail to find many
reasons and excuses for speech, nor will he fail to find a
person to whom to speak.

And a person given to such talkativeness is often motivat-
ed by a hidden desire to be known to all and to be the center of everyone's attention. The compulsive talker wastes
not his own time and attention only but also the time and
attention of those whom he chooses as his listeners.

Many excessively talkative people implicitly present
themselves as experts on all things, as if they are willing
and able to give advice to all other persons on all matters.
To point out and correct such a tendency (either in oneself
or in another person) is an undeniably difficult and painful
thing to do. Yet it is often more harmful to let this fault
pass uncorrected.

When Is Speaking at Length Useful and Helpful?

No one should imagine, though, that *all* extended discourse is inherently reprehensible or spiritually harmful. And this is able to be shown quite clearly out of the teachings and example of Christ Himself and the blessed apostles. For Christ, when He gave His great sermon on the mount, spoke to His disciples at considerable length.[5] And when He sent forth the twelve apostles, He likewise instructed them in detail in an extended discourse.[6] Finally, before He entered into His passion, after the last supper on the Thursday evening, He made a lengthy oration to His disciples. On that occasion, He spoke to them recognizing that they felt as if they were soon to be bereaved and orphaned, and He offered them golden words of encouragement and consolation.[7]

In a similar manner, we read that the apostle Paul once continued to speak to a group until the middle of the night for their edification in the Faith.[8] And comparable examples can be found amongst the early fathers of the Church. For example, Saint Anthony of Egypt often spoke to his monks at length on the life of prayer and

---

[5]   See Matthew 5.
[6]   See Matthew 10.
[7]   See John 14.
[8]   See Acts 20.

renunciation. And we read in the life of Saint Benedict how he once spent an entire night in conversation with his sister, Saint Scholastica, discussing the joys and glories of heaven. Wherever it shall be of particular and genuine usefulness or encouragement to another, speaking at some length may be esteemed as a work of charity and mercy.

Yet one should be extremely cautious in determining when lengthy discourse really is necessary or useful. Often, just as much can be said in a few carefully-chosen sentences than is conveyed in a long or elaborate sermon. Often, a discourse which would have been useful and edifying if kept brief becomes tedious and superfluous by being extended beyond measure. By avoiding unnecessary words, one can ensure that he always has something of value in reserve, ready to offer the brother or sister who really is in need of a word of wisdom or encouragement.

Hence it was that David said, in the previously quoted psalm, "Place, O Lord, a guard over my mouth, and set a secure gate at my lips."[9] Now a good guard is not only capable of keeping the mouth closed lest any foolish or wicked speech goes out from it, but it is also fully capable of opening the mouth when charity and good judgment genuinely require it.

---

[9] Psalm 141:3.

A Word of Caution against Excessive Rigor or Singularity in the Observance of Silence[10]

Hence, one must be cautious that one is not silent in a rigid or excessive way, especially amongst the people with whom one lives and works. For the person who cultivates silence excessively or imprudently will soon fall out of harmony with his community and colleagues. Through inordinate introspection, or through the snares of the devil, such a person often falls into dangerous vices and temptations. I myself have seen many such cases and have heard of many more. And you, my friend, probably know of such unfortunate instances yourself!

The one who makes wise and healthy religious resolutions does not concentrate simply on commencing his resolutions with great fervor and enthusiasm but rather on maintaining them in a sustainable manner so that they lead to a positive spiritual result in the long-term. Often, those who begin something more strictly than all their confreres end up by being more lax than anyone else! For they attempt to follow their chosen observance to an immoderate

---

[10] "Singularity" is a term used in religious life when a person does something which sets him apart in a conspicuous way from the general community. Often this singularity was something which may have been meritorious in itself (like additional observances of fasts, prayers, silence, etc.) but which causes division in the community.

or injudicious degree, generally without the counsel or approval of their superiors. And it is often not long before they find the burden they are trying to carry to be insupportable and cast it off altogether.[11]

Singular or individual observances are always a danger in communal settings, and fervor is more praiseworthy when it is in accordance with the practices and customs of one's community. It is, therefore, better to observe all the common rules and observances of one's religious house perfectly and without fault than to invent new and singular observances as an individual.

Silence and Speech for People in Different States of Life

There are some who consider it a very great thing if a person learns to maintain strict silence, and it cannot be denied that this does reflect truly a very meritorious discipline and dedication. Nevertheless, it is an even better thing if one can either keep silence or talk as is most befitting the particular circumstance. The person who lives as a hermit

---

[11] The point which Thomas is making here is reflected in the Rule of Benedict and other monastic and religious rules, which require members of the community to obtain permission and approval from the superior before any private spiritual, devotional, or penitential undertaking. His comments also apply to Christians in other states of life— namely, that one should exercise prudence and moderation in taking up spiritual or ascetic practices.

is able to keep very strict silence according to his own plan and disposition. The person who lives in a religious community or monastery should keep silence at appropriate times but also has permission to speak at times. And to speak with others in an appropriate way is not merely a right for such a person but, in fact, a duty demanded of him by charity, courtesy, and fraternity.

For the person living in the world and following a secular vocation, it is much harder to keep silence than for those in consecrated life, yet it is still possible at times. For those who live in the world and deal with secular business, they should be particularly cautious. For the obligations of constant conversation which fall upon many people in business and the professions make it very difficult not to slip into profane, worldly, or sinful words at times. Negligence and tolerance of profane speech quickly springs up, unless one keeps constant vigilance. Alas, it very often happens that a person who deals with worldly people and worldly business finds himself saying, as if unintentionally, things which he would have formerly blushed even to hear![12]

---

[12] This observation seems to be based on a comment made by Saint Gregory the Great in one of his homilies on the prophet Ezekiel: "Moreover, in my position, I must often communicate with worldly people. At times, I let my tongue run too freely, for if I am always severe in my judgments, the worldly will avoid me, and then I could never admonish them as I should. As a result, I often listen patiently to chatter. And because I too am weak, I find myself drawn little by little into idle conversation, and I begin to talk freely about matters which once I would have avoided altogether. What once I found tedious, I now enjoy!"

Some Particular Spiritual Snares Associated with Prolonged Conversations

There are many potential spiritual snares which lurk in the custom of holding long conversations with other people. Hence it is expedient here to offer some particular warnings.

For a person to indulge in frequent long conversations often tends to turn his attention away from religion and faith. Constant interaction with others can make time spent in the solitude of prayer and contemplation seem to be dry and tedious. And it is very rare to find any spiritual edification to result from a prolonged colloquy. Indeed, unless there is a particular topic which is being discussed and a particular purpose for discussing it, it is almost inevitable that the conversation will slip into frivolity, or murmuring, or gossip if it is sufficiently prolonged.

One should be particularly attentive to this in the morning and evening of the day. For these are the times when one should focus most on recollection and reflection. Those who permit themselves to enter into inane and profitless matters at the beginning and ending of the day will generally find that such matters occupy them during the rest of the day too!

Monks, nuns, and religious have a traditional practice of keeping strict silence after night prayer, and then maintaining this silence until their morning devotions are completed. This is a laudable practice which could be easily and very usefully imitated by all Christians, regardless of their state of life.

The Dangers of Speaking Late into the Night

It is a most deplorable custom to stay awake during the hours of the night in order to listen to gossip, fables, and speculation. Such a practice is not only harmful during the night concerned but often has real consequences the next day, such as tiredness or oversleeping. And the content of such nocturnal confabulations (whatever it might be) is hardly likely to be conducive to purity of heart or piety of intention. For any conversation which seeks to conceal itself in the darkness and secrecy of the night cannot be edifying or wholesome. As Aristotle once wisely declared, "From one fault, many others spring up." This is an exemplary case of that principle.

In effect, this practice of staying awake into the night to speak is not only taking time away from sleep but also (because of the resulting fatigue and distraction) effectively stealing from the God-given hours of work. Moreover, it affects not only the persons wishing to enter into this wicked vice but also others, whom it also deprives of rest and quietness. Thus it is truly a grave sin against both God and one's neighbors.[13]

Bad Experiences Springing from Late-Night Conversations

Many people have related to me how the practice of participating in conversations into the late hours of the night has given them very little entertainment or happiness but a disproportionate amount of disturbance and sorrow, and burdened their consciouses for many years into the future. For even if the first intention of the conversation is completely good and pure, it is generally not long before the forces of darkness and evil (which are always more restless at night) came to exert their pressure, and little by little to creep into one's words and thoughts.

And it often happens that something indecent or profane or scandalous is said quite incidentally. While such things may seem trivial or of little consequence at the time they are uttered, they often are absorbed deeply into the heart and leave impure or wicked thoughts which cannot easily be erased or removed. We human beings

---

[13] The words of Thomas are particularly strict and severe here. It seems likely that he is reflecting on his own experiences in religious life when he makes this warning against late-night conversation.

are fragile creatures, and it takes but one evil word or thought to leave a lasting stain on our heart or to wound our virtue. Let us not say or hear anything in the darkness which we would not want to be said or heard from the rooftops![14]

Some Advice on Avoiding Conversations Which Damage Virtue

A good strategy for escaping conversations which are potentially damaging to virtue and purity of heart is to avoid carefully the occasions when such conversations are likely to occur.[15] In this way, you will not give the flame of profanity the slightest chance to spring up.

For the undisciplined or poorly controlled tongue is like a flaming spear in the hands of the devil. It is this ancient enemy of the soul who is so often at work, and as soon as a person ceases to control his own tongue, the devil is waiting to take control of it himself for his own nefarious purposes!

---

[14] See Luke 12:3.

[15] Avoiding occasions for profane conversation might mean avoiding talking to particular individuals or groups of persons, or avoiding certain times or settings for conversations. The advice of Thomas is consistent with the practice of monastic and religious houses at the time, which generally permitted certain times of conversation and recreation when the whole community was present but discouraged private socialization beyond these designated times.

Necessary Speech

It cannot be denied that there are many occasions when speech is necessary. This includes communication concerning work and practical matters, and also speaking about spiritual perplexities and experiences. Human beings, by their very nature, require at times the counsel or consolation of their brothers or sisters.

Nevertheless, even when conversation is truly necessary, it should not be excessively prolonged, nor should it become too frequent. There are a great many who fall into excessive talkativeness, all the while deceiving themselves that every word they say is somehow indispensably necessary!

On Turning to God Alone

There are certain persons who, through the grace of faith and devotion, are able to turn to God alone for everything they need. In whatever doubts and perplexities they experience, they seek guidance and consolation not through human channels but through prayer and contemplation. Whenever they sense their soul to be stained by some shadow of vice or uncertainty, they commit the matter entirely to the kind providence and goodness of the almighty Lord.

Indeed, whatever wisdom and encouragement we seem to receive from human beings really comes from God alone.

How wise it is, therefore, to turn to God directly, since He is the one source of all our help!

By avoiding all conversations, beyond those which practical necessity or charity and courtesy demand, a person protects himself from innumerable occasions and instances of sin. And, what is more, by virtue of the fact that he does not participate in the exchange of superfluous and vain words, he also preserves others from the occasions of slipping.

A CONSIDERATION FOR THE WISE

It is good to bear in mind that a person will seldom be able to restrain himself from what is superfluous and harmful until he also develops the discipline to restrain himself from what is licit and innocuous at times, and thereby learn true self-control. The wise person will come to realize that few words are sufficient, and much (or even most) that is said is unnecessary and useless. And the garrulousness of the multitude will become utterly alien and tedious to him.

But to the foolish, any number of words will never be enough to satisfy them, neither will they be able to imitate the restraint and self-control of the wise. Nevertheless, what is written in Scripture remains absolutely true: "If a fool remain silent, he shall be considered a wise man."[16]

---

[16] Proverbs 17:28.

The Difficulties of People Who Are in the Habit of Unrestrained Speech

However, even if the fool wished to put into practice this advice about the cultivation of silence, he should find it difficult to maintain for very long. For those who are accustomed to idle chatter, to remain quiet for any length of time seems like an arduous and even impossible task.

Indeed, they may come to recognize how much of their conversation has been filled with vacuous and empty matters, and how much useless verbiage they produce. They may even sincerely repent, with unfeigned tears and sighs, for this habitual weakness. Yet very often, as soon as the occasion presents itself, they will fall into precisely the same behavior as before and revert to their former talkativeness!

How an Excessively Talkative Person Can Correct Himself

But if anyone firmly resolves to correct the habit of unrestrained speech or excessive talkativeness, he should renew each day this intention, committing himself to it for the love of Christ and imploring His assistance. Furthermore, he should studiously avoid all occasions when he knows he is likely to become talkative. In particular, he should avoid having private or long conversations with any people with whom he was formerly accustomed to share gossip or idle chatter.

A person who is excessively talkative should undertake to correct himself not only because loquaciousness and lack of control of the tongue is a vice in itself but also because it gives rise to so many other sins. An unrestrained tongue is the source of a whole multitude of wickedness and evil. And it is rebellious and difficult to control. "No human being is able to tame the tongue," as the apostle James wrote.[17]

This pronouncement is a grave lamentation and indictment of our mortal weakness and debility—that the human being, with all his wisdom and intelligence, cannot succeed in bringing the organ of speech under control.

And often it is much easier to be completely silent than to achieve proper moderation and restraint, and to avoid saying that which is foolish or flippant. Indeed, how many snares and stumbling blocks could a person avoid simply by holding his peace!

The Multitude of Vices Which Appear in Speech

Who can fully judge or comprehend just how many and varied are the sins and vices which come to being through our words?

---

[17] James 3:8.

Let us ask ourselves, how often are our words:

- pointless and profitless,
- flippant and foolish,
- fatuous and fallacious,
- proud and presumptuous,
- cruel and cold,
- angry and aggressive,
- dissolute and dissipated,
- lustful and lascivious,
- vainglorious and vapid,
- detracting and demeaning,
- mendacious and misleading,
- scandalous and scurrilous,
- dishonest and deceptive,
- hurtful and harmful,
- superfluous and senseless,
- illicit and ill-timed,
- unlawful and ungoverned, or
- impure and improvident?[18]

The honest answer is, alas, almost each and every time we open our mouths!

---

[18] In the original Latin text, all of the listed adjectives rhyme—a feat which is clearly impossible to replicate in English. The present rendering is a free adaptation designed to emulate something of the effect of the original. All of the original ideas of Thomas are included but have been rearranged to achieve the alliteration.

THE VICE OF DETRACTION

Amongst all of those vices listed above, detraction is often seen to be the most common. Detraction is the practice of speaking critically about people who are absent, and it is very prevalent in communal settings of all kinds. Often, each person present will say whatever it is that pleases or displeases them about another person, who (of course) is not there to hear them or defend himself. This leads then to a lack of restraint and prudence. How often when we speak about others we say things which, as soon as we have uttered them, we regret we ever said! But, alas, our words, once said, can never be retracted or revoked.

Let us learn from our mistakes. If we have slipped once, let us be on our guard not to slip in the same way a second time.

HOW EASY IT IS TO SIN IN OUR WORDS AND OUR HEARTS

In what do we sin more easily than in our words? "The one who never stumbles or offends in his words may be regarded as a perfect human being."[19]

Nevertheless, it is true to say that perhaps we sin even more easily in our thoughts than in our words, and we often sin more gravely in thought than speech. "It is out of

---

[19] James 3:2.

the heart," declared the Lord, "that blasphemies and lies arise—everything that renders a person impure."[20] For evil is first conceived in the heart, and a wicked word proceeds from a wicked heart. But our sins committed in the heart are hidden and often unknown, whereas our sins committed in speech are public and cannot be concealed or denied. Hence it is wisely written, "In much speaking, you cannot avoid sin."[21]

How a Person Can Be Deceived and Retracted from the Good Intention of Cultivating Restraint of Speech

Often, a person makes a good resolution to cultivate restraint of speech and to practice silence at certain times. But then he is deceived by temptation and (for the apparent sake of affability or charity) he falls away from his good intention. Many people who wish to correct the fault of excessive talkativeness also fear that they will be seen to be going too much to the other extreme by becoming unnecessarily taciturn. Through this, they consider that they may fail in their duty of fraternal charity. This is indeed a commendable sentiment in itself, for charity is of much higher value than mere silence. Refusing a kind word to a person in genuine

---

[20] Matthew 15:19–20.
[21] Proverbs 10:19.

need of one amounts to a sin and an act of negligence. And it is written that "a good word is better than any gift."[22]

In this way, it very often happens that a person will soon compromise his original intention of cultivating restraint of speech. This first compromise is certainly not a sin but rather virtue. Nevertheless, it happens all too often that after the first such compromise, the second will be made more readily, and then the third will be readier yet. Then any excuse, however slight, will be seen to suffice as a valid reason for breaking silence. And in this way, the person is soon completely drawn away from his original intention of cultivating restraint of speech and reverts to his former habits.

If anyone experiences this and finds himself in the situation described above, it behooves him to acknowledge his own fault honestly and without dissimulation. He should examine himself carefully to recognize at what point charity ceased to be his only motivation and his own proclivity to talkativeness began to govern him (or at least to influence him). When he is able to recognize this clearly, he will be much better equipped to recommence his first good resolution to cultivate silence.[23]

---

[22] Sirach 18:17.

[23] From this point, the text of Thomas becomes slightly fragmented, with apparently accidental repetition of certain ideas. Some minor abridgements have been made from here onwards, and certain extremely short chapters of Thomas have been joined together, for the sake of readability.

Applying Discretion in Everything Which Has Been Recommended

It is, of course, necessary that a person applies wise discretion in applying everything which has been said so far. The spiritual benefits of silence and the spiritual perils of loquacity have been described in detail. Reflecting upon these will assist the lover of virtue to proceed with all circumspection and prudence.

But it would be wrong to commend silence in a complete and absolute sense, as if it were ideal that it should be continually preserved under all circumstances. Similarly, it would be foolish to condemn all speech and conversation, for, while it has many perils, it also carries many possible benefits and blessings.

The most beautiful of all the virtues is discretion. For this virtue shows to the soul the most perfect path on which to travel towards true sanctity and charity, instructing it to beware of the snares which lie both to the right and to the left of that narrow and sacred path.

As a Whole, We Need to Cultivate Silence More than Speech

As a whole, humanity needs to cultivate silence more than speech. There are some people who need to be encouraged to speak more, but these are few and rare. On the other hand, there are very many who talk to excess, without restraint and prudence. For to speak and gossip is in accordance with our lower nature, but to keep silence is to run contrary to the tendency of the flesh. For the flesh incessantly seeks consolations and entertainment in the things of the exterior world rather than in the things of the spirit.

At certain times in life, however, human beings do tend to become silent. This is on those occasions when we are most deeply touched, when our hearts are pierced with love or awe. And this is surely the best way to be in the presence of God.

For those who have received this grace of silence, let them take care to cultivate it carefully and not let it succumb to the distracting impulses of the flesh and the world.

Why We Sometimes Fail to Find Spiritual Consolations

If we find that we are lacking interior and spiritual consolations and satisfaction in our life, it is quite often a sign that we are trying too intently to derive satisfaction from the things of the exterior world. As long as we are intent on finding consolation in human and passing things, we shall be neither worthy nor ready to receive divine and heavenly joys.

Of course, it is difficult to renounce the desire for worldly, human, and exterior satisfactions and consolations altogether. If a person finds this impossible, he should attempt to reduce his need and desire for these things little by little and step by step. And renouncing lower things in this way, his heart will be more and more directed to that which is higher.

How the Devil Often Strives to Impede Devotion to God through Sadness and Boredom

The devil is the sworn foe of the human race and envies in particular any person who develops a close relationship to God. Therefore, he seldom permits such a person to go long without testing him with some trial or temptation. For this reason, the devout person needs to be especially vigilant against the attacks of the devil.

Very often, the ancient enemy will send bursts of serious sadness or dark depression, as well as tedium and boredom. Above all, he is intent upon subverting the commitment and resolve of those who have dedicated themselves to a contemplative life of silence and solitude. The vices he uses against such people are sadness and boredom so that tedium and frustration soon begin to arise in their hearts. As many persons drawn to the solitary life are of a naturally melancholic temperament, the devil cunningly exploits this. He sends oppressive and consuming sorrows in an attempt to drain the person of all his resolve and strength.

But whoever firmly believes in God and places the love of God above all else, and honestly desires to conquer the world and the pernicious lusts of the world, shall have the courage and endurance to accept all affliction of bitterness, sorrow, and tedium. He shall neither seek nor expect any solace from human beings or any created things but will be inflamed with a desire for Christ alone. For in Christ he will see the only one who is able to be victorious not only over sadness and tedium but over all the vices and temptations which the devil might send him, and to lead him unfailingly to the glories of heaven.

STRENGTH AND COURAGE ARE NEEDED TO OVERCOME THE ENEMY

The one who is strong and courageous in the Lord may experience temptations and be assaulted by many and varied attacks by the devil. Yet in the end, such a person shall be able to fight successfully against his enemy, armed with the invincible shield of true faith. And what can I say of those holy souls who refuse to allow such unclean spirits to enter over their threshold? How blessed they are, and what celestial delights are theirs!

But there are, alas, those who all too readily succumb to sadness and boredom. Even if they possess the spiritual weapons with which to fight, they are often too lethargic to make proper use of them. Their heart can then grow discouraged and dejected so that they surrender to the wicked promptings of the foe without even confronting him in battle.

Therefore, O soldier of Christ, clothe yourself in strength and courage! Do not be discouraged by every passing cloud or shadow of melancholy or tedium. Do not become afraid at the rustling of falling leaves or the blowing of mere breezes! Rather, stand ready to fight the devil, and give no credence to his wicked suggestions. The all-powerful Lord Himself shall be your guardian and protector, and the spiritual reward you will receive shall be truly magnificent! It is God's power alone which shall permit you to conquer the waverings, distractions, and caprices of your own heart, and God shall not fail to impart that power to you.

Now I, who have set out to speak about restraint of speech, have myself spoken excessively and at too great a length. It behooves me, therefore, to return now to my own safe harbor of silence. Let the tongue which has spoken and the hand which has been writing these words now together enjoy the blessed and tranquil rest of quiet and stillness. And may God be blessed in all things. Amen.

OF THE LOVE OF SOLITUDE AND SILENCE[1]

Seek a proper time to retire into thyself, and often think of the benefits of God.

Let curiosities alone.

Read such matters as may rather move thee to compunction than give thee occupation.

If thou wilt withdraw thyself from superfluous talk and idle visits, as also from giving ear to news and to reports, thou wilt find time sufficient and proper to employ thyself in good meditations.

The greatest saints avoided the company of men as much as they could and chose to live to God in secret.

2. "As often as I have been amongst men," said a philosopher, "I have returned less a man"; this we often experience when we talk long.

---

[1] This chapter is an excerpt from *The Imitation of Christ* by Thomas à Kempis.

It is easier to be altogether silent than not to exceed in words.

It is easier to keep retired at home than to be able to be sufficiently upon one's guard abroad.

Whosoever, therefore, aims at arriving at internal and spiritual things, must, with Jesus, go aside from the crowd. (*John* 5:13).

No man is secure in appearing abroad, but he who would willingly lie hid at home.

No man securely speaks but he who loves to hold his peace.

No man securely governs but he who would willingly live in subjection.

No man securely commands but he who has learned well to obey.

3. No man securely rejoiceth unless he hath within him the testimony of a good conscience. (*2 Cor.* 1:12).

Yet the security of the saints was always full of the fear of God.

Neither were they less careful or humble in themselves, because they were shining with great virtues and graces.

But the security of the wicked arises from pride and presumption, and will end in deceiving themselves.

Never promise thyself security in this life, though thou seem to be a good religious man, or a devout hermit.

4. Oftentimes they that were better in the judgment of men have been in greater danger by reason of their too great confidence.

So that it is better for many not to be altogether free from temptations but to be often assaulted; that they may not be too secure lest, perhaps, they be lifted up with pride, or take more liberty to go aside after exterior comforts.

Oh, how good a conscience would that man preserve, who would never seek after transitory joy, nor ever busy himself with the world!

Oh, how great peace and tranquillity would he possess, who would cut off all vain solicitude, and only think of the things of God, and his salvation, and place his whole hope in God!

5. No man is worthy of heavenly comfort who has not diligently exercised himself in holy compunction.

If thou wouldst find compunction in thy heart retire into thy chamber and shut out the tumult of the world, as it is written: "Have compunction in your chambers." (*Ps.* 4:5). Thou shalt find in thy cell what thou shalt often lose abroad.

Thy cell, if thou continue in it, grows sweet; but if thou keep not to it, it becomes tedious and distasteful. If in the beginning of thy conversion thou accustom thyself to remain in thy cell and keep it well, it will be to thee afterwards a dear friend and a most agreeable delight.

6. In silence and quiet the devout soul goes forward and learns the secrets of the Scriptures.

There she finds floods of tears, with which she may wash and cleanse herself every night, that she may become the more familiar with her Maker, by the farther she lives from all worldly tumult. (*Ps.* 6).

For God with His holy angels will draw nigh to him who withdraws himself from his acquaintances and friends.

It is better to lie hidden and take care of one's self than neglecting one's self to work even miracles.

It is commendable for a religious man to go seldom abroad, to fly being seen, and not desire to see men.

7. Why wilt thou see what thou must not have? "The world passeth away, and the concupiscence thereof." (*1 John* 2:17).

The desires of sensuality draw thee abroad, but when the hour is past what dost thou bring home but a weight upon thy conscience and a dissipation of heart.

A joyful going abroad often brings forth a sorrowful coming home; and a merry evening makes a sad morning.

So all carnal joys enter pleasantly but in the end bring remorse and death.

What canst thou see elsewhere which thou seest not here? Behold the heavens and the earth, and all the elements; for of these are all things made.

8. What canst thou see anywhere which can continue long under the sun?

Thou thinkest perhaps to be satisfied, but thou canst not attain to it.

If thou couldst see all things at once before thee what would it be but a vain sight? (*Eccles.* 1:14).

Lift up thine eyes to God on high and pray for thy sins and negligences. (*Eccles.* 3:4; *Ps.* 122:1).

Leave vain things to vain people, but mind thou the things which God hath commanded thee.

Shut thy door upon thee, and call to thee Jesus thy beloved.

Stay with Him in thy cell, for thou shalt not find such great peace anywhere else.

If thou hadst not gone abroad, nor hearkened to rumors, thou hadst kept thyself better in good peace; but since thou art delighted sometimes to hear news thou must thence suffer a disturbance of heart.

Practcal Reflections

Exterior retirement is not sufficient to engage and satisfy a heart which would really withdraw itself from creatures to be occupied on itself alone, but interior retirement is likewise necessary, which is a spirit of recollection and prayer. A soul which is separated from all the amusements of the senses, seeks and finds in God that pure satisfaction which it can never meet with in creatures. A respectful and frequent remembrance of the presence of God occupies the mind, and an ardent desire of pleasing Him and of becoming worthy of His love engages the heart. It is absorbed in Him alone: all things else dwindle into nothing. It buries itself in its dear solitude, and dies to itself and all things in God: it breathes only His love, it forgets all to remember only Him; penetrated with grief for its infidelities it mourns incessantly in His pressure, it sighs continually for the pleasure of seeing and possessing Him in Heaven, it nourishes itself with reading good books, and with the exercise of prayer, it is never tired of treating with God on the affairs of salvation, at least it humbly supports the irksomeness it may experience, and with a view of honoring His sovereign dominion by the complete destruction of sin in itself, it renounces all desire of finding any other satisfaction than that of pleasing Him.

PRAYER

O my God, when will silence, retirement, and prayer become the occupations of my soul, as they are now frequently the objects of my desires? How am I wearied with saying so much and yet doing so little for Thee! Come, Jesus, come, Thou the only object of my love, the center and supreme happiness of my soul! Come, and impress my mind with such a lively conviction of Thy presence that all within me may yield to its influence. Come, Lord, and speak to my heart, communicate to it Thy holy will, and mercifully work within it both to will and to do according to Thy good pleasure. Alas, how long shall my exile be prolonged? When shall the veil be removed which separates time from eternity? When shall I see that which I now believe? When shall I find what I seek? When shall I possess what I love, which is Thyself, O my God! Grant, O Jesus, that these holy desires with which Thou now inspirest me may be followed by that eternal happiness which I hope for from Thine infinite mercy. *Amen.*